STAFFORD CLIFF

1000 KITCHEN IDEAS

PHOTOGRAPHS BY CHRISTIAN SARRAMON

Quadrille
PUBLISHING

Introduction 10

Style and Function 12

Cooking and Eating 26

Country Kitchens 46

The City Kitchen 72

Storage Solutions 90

Light and Shade 108

Display Options 124

Walls and Floors 146

Texture and Colour 168

Fully Equipped 184

Quirks and Details 194

Acknowledgements 208

The kitchen of today should be renamed the living room. Not only is it the room you prepare and cook food in, but more than likely you eat in it too – or in a space adjacent to it. Cooking and eating can no longer be separated. More than any other room in your house, planning the kitchen involves many considerations in addition to the furniture: hygiene, safety, function, practicality, flexibility and aesthetics. Some kitchens will be constantly full of activity; some will be a singular retreat for quiet cooking or meals on the trot. What you have to begin with will dictate, to an extent, what you end up with – even if you have the luxury and the finances to start completely from scratch. The size and shape of the room, where the doors, windows and plumbing are, the height of the ceiling and so forth will all play a part. Doors and worktops are available in dozens of materials, finishes and colours, and the range of equipment has never been so varied. This probably makes it harder than ever to choose those that will fit your aesthetics and your budget. What you need to think about is how to make your kitchen individual: the finishing touches, even if they might come at the beginning – French doors, for instance, a roof light or under-floor heating. The best kitchens are those that reflect the personality of the owner, not the personality of the manufacturers. Start from the way you like to cook – in company or in private – and the other purposes you want the room to serve. Is it a family room, a place for entertaining friends or a spotless lifestyle statement and status symbol? A professional kitchen writer once provided a list of things that might take place in a kitchen. As well as cooking and eating, she included feeding pets, doing homework, watching TV, and making love. You may not have anticipated the latter, but if your room turns out to be seductive enough, who knows what will be on the menu?

STYLE AND

FUNCTION

When we start thinking about moving house, the thing that decisions most often hinge on is the size and style of kitchen. Is the new kitchen better than your current one in terms of size, shape and outlook? Do you know what size you want anyway? Does it include space to eat, nice windows, a door to a garden – or better still, a patio or deck? Is it a bright, cheerful space or a gloomy one? If the kitchen has been recently refitted, are the units and the equipment in the style you like, or will you want to rip everything out and start again? If it has what they call 'original fittings', are you up to the task and the cost involved in its transformation? You might be bringing your own furniture, but you are unlikely to move in with new kitchen furniture apart, that is, from a table and chairs and perhaps a kitchen dresser. So it's a good idea to decide what you are prepared to do to realise your dream. If the rest of your rooms are modern, do you want a modern kitchen too? And if so, do you want to fill it with state-of-the-art equipment? Sometimes it's easier to consider what it is you don't want. Start with the walls, floors and ceiling. You will probably want to eat in your kitchen, but if so, how many people do you want to seat, and how often? If you have a young family, they will bring their own demands. Finally – do you want to cook at all? Or are you like one famous NY theatre star who, when she moved into her new apartment, had the cooker removed, along with any temptation to use it.

COOKING

AND EATING

Whether you think of cooking as an art, a hobby, or a chore, there is an energy that is given off by the activity of preparing and serving food that is as primal as life itself. As a result, some of the most satisfying and joyful types of kitchens are those where cooking and eating take place in the same space; whether for a family lunch, friends for dinner, or even what you might call a special occasion. Gone are the days when houses had a room that was used only for such events. Many restaurants now have open views of the kitchen – so that you can watch and share in all the activity – and in some top-class establishments, the most sought after table is one sited in the kitchen itself. Removing the walls (and the secrecy of cooking that goes with them) heightens anticipation, stimulates tastebuds and makes the food taste better. The same is true at home. Doing the cooking and eating in the same space breaks down the barriers between the cook, the rest of the family, and other dinner guests – allowing for plenty of interaction, good and bad. In terms of the furniture, there are countless options for tables and chairs, from the island unit with pull-up stools, to the slide-out table and folding chairs, to the big wooden table with high back leather carvers; all at relatively affordable prices. If your diners feel so comfortable that the meal becomes relaxed and open-ended, and everyone is having a good time, what more can you ask from your décor?

COUNTRY
KITCHENS

Complete with muddy rubber boots by the back door and, from the windows, views of rolling countryside, no other style of room abounds with so much warmth and well-being, so much sense of history and tradition, as the country kitchen. These are our favourite rooms in farm museums and restored country houses. The materials used here are rustic and natural: stone, brick or tiles on the floor; beams on the ceiling and plenty of wood – either natural or painted. Where possible there may be an open fire, or an old chimney breast in which a traditional-style cooker has been fitted. Kitchen manufacturers see this vision too, and fulfil it with their ranges of Aga cookers, butler's sinks and cream-painted cupboard doors with mouldings and brass handles. In the country kitchen, everything is on display: paintings, children's drawings, plants, baskets, glassware, plates and jugs on open racks, and cooking utensils (especially if stainless steel, copper or enamel). The cupboards here have either glass-fronted doors or none at all, with ruched fabric curtains taking their place instead. Lighting tends to be traditional, with brass or iron fittings, and with its dog baskets, cat flaps, goldfish bowls or hamster wheels, this room is a home for animals too. But the most evocative item here has to be the produce – the baskets of vegetables and fresh-picked fruit, jars of homemade jam, maturing cheeses, cakes, scones, and most important of all, freshly baked bread.

THE CITY

KITCHEN

City kitchens tend to be defined more by their size and style than by their location. Whereas some rooms depend on being large for their impact and stylishness, a kitchen often has to fit into a small, compact space. With the ergonomic studies of the 1950s, it was found that the distance housewives had to walk to perform a simple kitchen task could be enormous. So the galley kitchen, in which you could stand in the middle and reach either side just by turning around, was invented. The concept of the 'work triangle' established the ideal position for the cooker, the fridge and the sink unit. Since then the space given to the kitchen in the home has become more generous and we have seen the invention of the island unit – which at first came complete with a 'breakfast bar' and has now evolved to include either a sink or a hob. 'Integrated' has become the buzzword, with state-of-the-art equipment all seamlessly concealed within bespoke cabinetry. While colour is important in the city kitchen, finish and materials – such as marble, glass or polished steel, as well as surfaces such as corian – are more so. Gone are the days when everything had to be straight- or square-sided. Cabinetry can now curve or bow, sinks can be round and hobs semi-circular. The modern city kitchen is sculptural, its fittings – whether a stylish modern cooker hood or a twin-door metallic and glass-fronted fridge – are designed to blend into a totemic whole, rather than being simply a jumble of mismatched bits.

STORAGE

SOLUTIONS

When planning a kitchen, perhaps one of the most important considerations is how much storage space is needed or wanted. If your idea of luxury is to have everything stored away out of sight, there are now some ingenious solutions available. You will find shelves that rotate out from normally inaccessible corners, as well as drawers for storing every piece of equipment or utensil, cup or bowl. Many traditional kitchens include a cupboard like an old Welsh dresser, a breakfront or a china cabinet, and in Germany, France and Scandinavia in the 16th and 17th centuries, housewares were kept in beautifully carved or hand-painted cupboards that are still highly prized today. The tradition of a bespoke cupboard to store kitchenware can be traced back as far as the 7th century Japanese Tansu. More recent storage inspiration also comes from 19th century grocery stores — where all of the most popular wares were stocked on simple wall-to-wall wooden shelves, or in below-waist-height drawers and cupboards. Many of these original fittings are recycled and turn up in kitchens today. Fitted kitchens did not arrive until the 1950's. When manufacturers introduced the first 'modern' kitchen cabinet in the 1920's, it was a stand-alone unit that came complete with an enamel-covered work surface (for pastry rolling), integrated spice and egg racks, storage jars, towel rail, fold-down ironing board and shopping list reminder, as well as a nifty component for sifting flour.

LIGHT AND

SHADE

Somebody once said that a kitchen should be as spotless as an operating theatre. In order to achieve this, your kitchen will have to borrow one of the theatre's most important features – its very efficient lighting. Lighting a room can be a real art form, as important in daytime as at night, and should be divided into two types; task lighting and mood lighting. At its most basic you should have light in front of you, focused on the areas where you will be working. After that, there are hundreds of sizes and types of light fitting available – tiny halogen, tungsten and LED fittings, most of which can be set into, onto or under every surface. There is no excuse for a dark corner. And yet, at the same time, you don't want to blast your kitchen with light – you're not cooking in a television studio after all. You will want a bit of variety of light and shade; some pools and sparkles and highlights in places. You will need some flexibility too: bright cheerful light for breakfast on a grey morning, moody atmospheric effects for a 'kitchen supper' with friends. Then there is the showy fashionable aspect to lighting – chandeliers are now surprisingly popular in kitchens, particularly hanging over a dining table or an island unit. These range from old-fashioned brass fittings and elaborate crystal creations to modern designs resembling exotic blooms or jelly fish; the most innovative of which are composed of fragments of broken china, or clusters of tiny recycled plastic bottles.

DISPLAY

OPTIONS

Stylistically kitchens seem to fall into two categories, cluttered or minimal. I don't mean cluttered as in 'messy' or 'untidy' (though kitchens can certainly pass through that phase) and I don't mean minimal as in empty or uninteresting. Minimal kitchens are generally modern and city-based, with everything hidden behind beautiful tailor-made hydraulically opening and closing doors and drawers. Cluttered kitchens are where we see display, and over the next few pages, you'll find plenty of it. Essentially the concept depends on open-fronted shelves, on which cooking and eating wares are stored. Things as beautiful as they are useful; that is one of the unique elements of cookware – both old and new – it can look great. Groups of cooking pans, utensils, cutlery, glassware and old baskets all look wonderful. This stuff is called 'kitchenalia' and can, if it's not inherited, be found by the discerning collector in antique fairs, flea markets and yard sales around the world. For every type of object – from tea caddies to toasters, kettles to coffee pots – there is a group of people who collect it, swap it, talk about it, and adore it. But certain things wear better than others. Plates, tureens, glasses and tinware look fine and can all be put to good use, but wooden chopping boards, salad bowls and old brushes are best kept just for admiring. If any of these things on display gathers a bit of dust between uses, don't worry. That too has a name. It's called patina!

WALLS AND

FLOORS

These are the aspects of the kitchen where most people prefer to use materials that are of a traditional nature. Generally speaking, the most permanent materials are the most desirable and the most expensive. You might be lucky enough to inherit a wonderful floor of old flagstones, terracotta tiles, brick or pebbles. On the other hand, these surfaces can be pretty unforgiving on the feet if you spend a long time standing, whereas cork, rubber, linoleum and various types of wood can be cheaper and easier to lay, as well as being softer and quieter to pad about on, and more child friendly too. A lot will depend on where you live, the type of house, and the style of the kitchen furniture you plan. Traditional floors suit traditional kitchens and 'modern' materials such as slate, tile, or sheet metal, suit modern schemes. Colour also plays a part – natural earth tones versus grey, silver, white or black. Colourful patterns can be fun, but take care not to choose something that you might grow tired of. Better to save extravagant excesses for curtains, roller blinds or tablecloths. When it comes to walls, tiled surfaces are practical, especially near the cooker or sink – and there are plenty of sizes, colours and patterns to choose from. Finally, look at what you have already and consider taking away, rather than adding. Exposed brickwork, raw plaster or tongue-and-groove timber can sometimes be the unexpected solution for adding the wow factor.

TEXTURE

AND COLOUR

After the moody lighting, gleaming pans, gurgling coffee maker and smoothly closing drawers, the next really sensual aspects of the kitchen are colour and texture – or at least they can be. Consider the semi-reflective finish of metal fridges or worktops, the look and touch of natural teak or oak; the gloss of ceramic tiles. This is just the beginning. Manufacturers of worktops are producing dozens of man-made composite surfaces – from granite to glass, concrete to stainless steel, and even some made out of coconut husks and seashells. A number, like corian, can be seamlessly moulded into any size, shape or colour, while others, like high gloss or matt lacquer, have the deep sheen of seven coats. There are also lots of sustainable wood veneers to choose from, without destroying any rainforests in the process, or you could commission a local craftsman or cabinet maker to create something uniquely for you. Colour in the kitchen is not forgotten, but choosing a work surface is like choosing new china – you need to think first about how food will look on it. Perhaps most remarkable of all are the three-dimensional textures now available. Suitable for walls or ceilings, they transform any surface into a folding geometric or rippling cascade as sinuous as a sand dune or as slinky as a Fortuny fabric. Etched into MDF board and coated with a foil membrane, they bring the computer age, art world and fashion catwalk right into the heart of the kitchen.

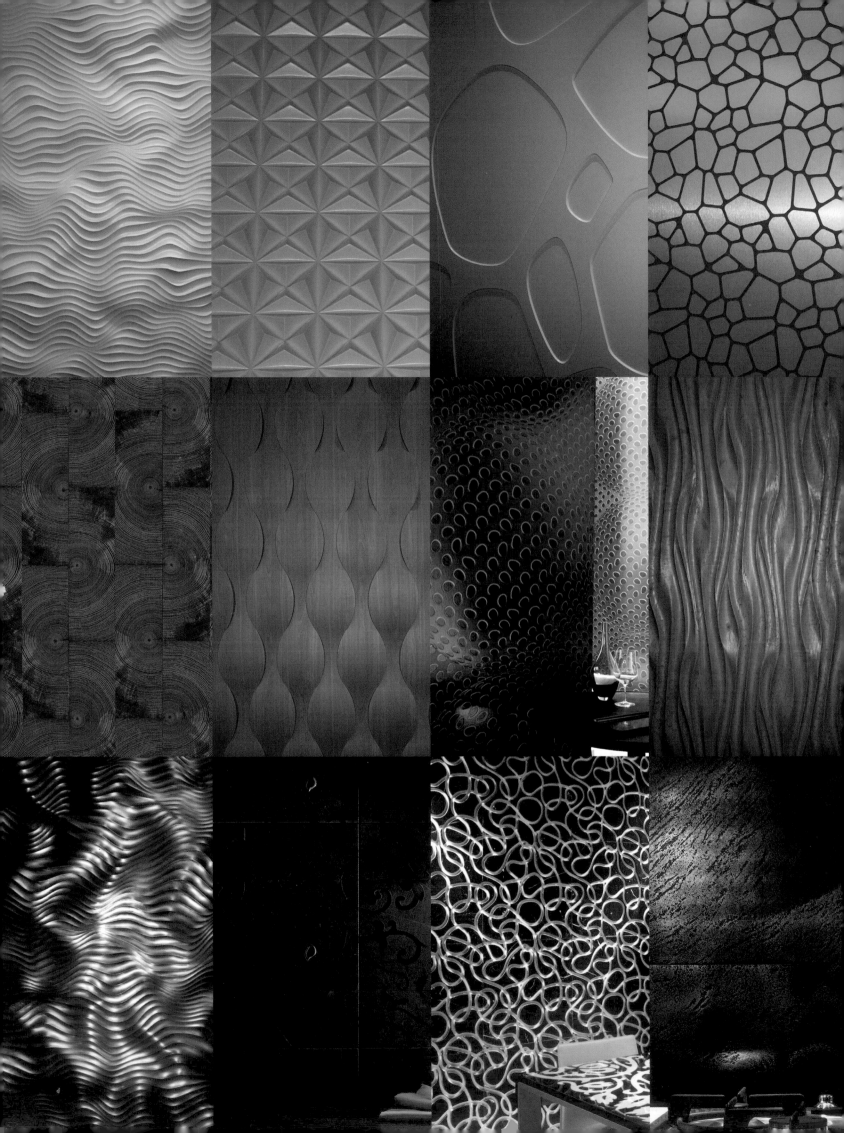

If you haven't been to visit a kitchen showroom recently, you might be surprised to discover that some amazing things have been happening. Of course, they still sell cookers, hobs and sinks, but the technology has changed. As well as gas or electric, you can now get steam ovens, and even ovens with shelves which – when you put in your chicken or turkey and press 'roast', 'bake' or 'broil' – automatically weigh the bird and calculate the correct cooking time. Available in black or white glass, flush-mounted induction hobs feel cool to the touch and only transfer heat to metal objects like cooking pans, whilst a teppanyaki is a heated flat metal plate set into the work surface, on which you can stir- or pan-fry. Everything in today's kitchen, even the coffee machine, can come fully-integrated. Extractors can be found concealed in various designs of chandelier, while taps are available with all sorts of flexible nozzles, including one that hides a tiny LED light inside the spout. You can, if you wish, have ice-cold filtered drinking water in one tap, and instant 100°C boiling water in another. Drawers are available for everything, including warming plates, dishwashers and freezers. You can even have drawers within drawers, most with sensual, soft-closing mechanisms. Finally, according to one manufacturer's marketing ploy – fridges have now 'disappeared' and have been replaced by state-of-the-art climate-controlled 'freshness centres'!

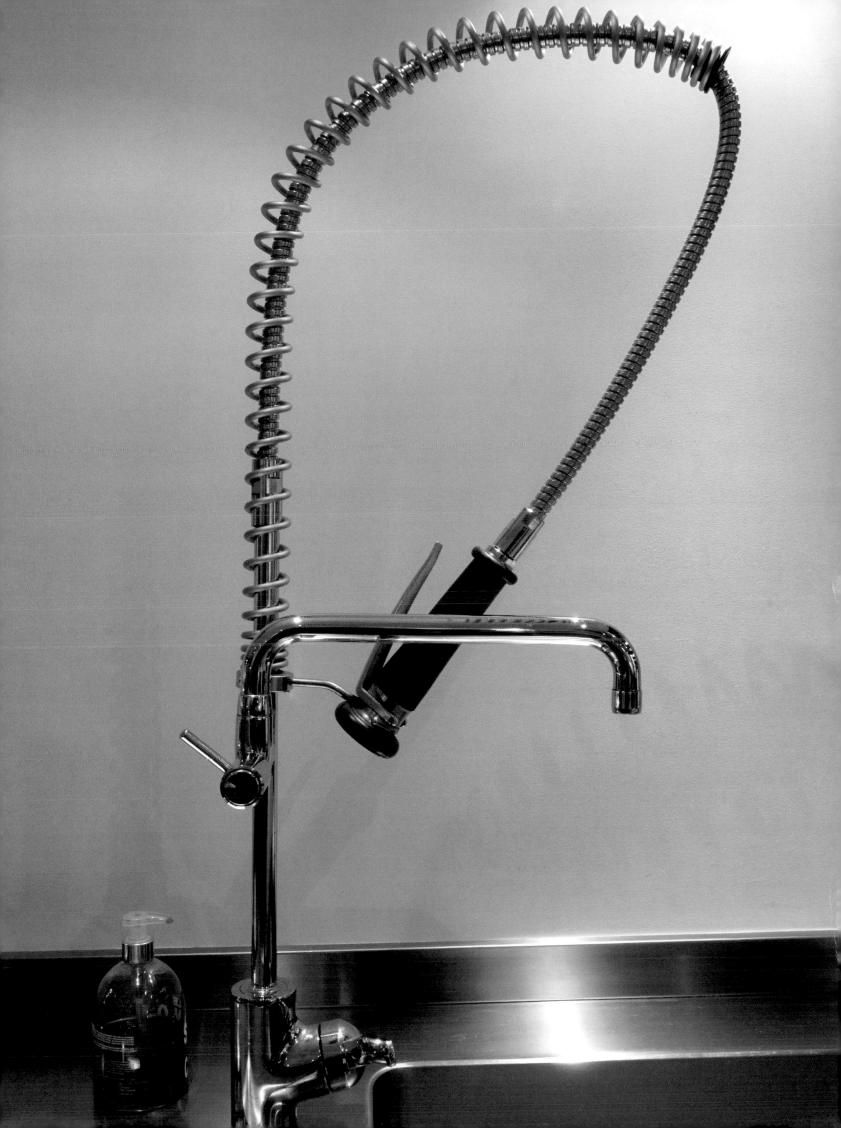

QUIRKS AND

DETAILS

At first glance, you might think that many of the ingredients and the ideas in this last chapter are pretty frivolous and, to an extent, you would be right. Bird cages, stuffed animals, nostalgic posters, framed prints, paintings and drawings – clusters, arrangements and collections of objects. The sort of things that are scattered throughout the other pages of this book. And yet, it is these objects that make your kitchen unique and personal. These are the things that attract your eye when you first walk into a room. They tell stories. They show passion, history and love. Even kitchen utensils and cooking equipment can be interesting to look at – particularly if they are antique pottery, decorative enamelware or modern design icons. The kitchen is a room full of activity that involves the whole family – so children's drawings, collages, cardboard constructions, sports awards or holiday-collected treasures can all be found here, as can postcards and photographs. Less visible are the many practical quirks and details that make up the storage components inside the kitchen's cupboards: the cutlery drawers, bread bins, herb and spice containers, vegetable trays, plate racks, saucepan drawers and segregated waste disposal bins. In the super-modern kitchen, most below-counter doors have been replaced by smoothly-sliding drawers, which make stooping and searching in dark recesses a thing of the past. Not so frivolous after all!

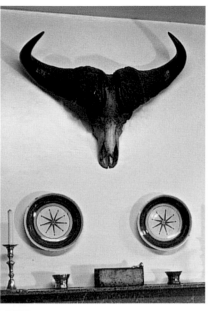

Acknowledgements

If the kitchen is the hub of the home, then the spokes are the link to every part of our lives. Memories are made in the kitchen as well as food. As you have seen, function is the most important aspect of this room, but for everything to work it has to look good and give you aesthetic pleasure too. There are many more than 1000 ideas in this book, so trust your instinct to tell you what is right for you. Like a bird making a nest, choose the bits that you like, add a few of your own, and the chances are that – like a recipe handed down from one generation to another – it will give you great pleasure for many years to come. **Stafford Cliff, London**

The kitchens on these pages are the loving creations of many people around the world, and I would like to thank all those who, over the last twenty years, have opened their doors and welcomed me into their homes so that I could see their many treasures.
I would also like to express my warmest appreciation to all the architects, designers, decorators, stylists, journalists and assistants who were essential on the photographic shoots. Thanks also to Xavie'z, Matthieu Moarovani Designer, Galerie La Cornue and Boffi for allowing me to use their beautiful things.
Many special thanks to Stafford Cliff, who has produced a brilliant design from my modest photographs.
To Jane O'Shea for her enthusiasm and kindness. And, of course, thanks to my wife Inès, and my two sons, Diego and Kim, for their help and endless patience each day.
Christian Sarramon, Paris

Manufacturers' details
Page 40 bottom right; page 41 top centre and right, bottom left; page 82 bottom left; page 90 top left and top middle left; page 175 bottom left; page 179 bottom; page 188 top left; page 202 top left, centre four; page 203 top right, centre four pictures: **Newcastle Furniture** is a bespoke kitchen design company that has built a solid reputation founded on quality and outstanding professionalism.
Tel: +44 (0) 1912 618900;
www.newcastlefurniture.com

Page 81 top; page 118 top; page 202 top right and bottom right: **Harvey Jones** is a leading retailer of handmade kitchens synonymous with premium quality and beautiful design, using the finest materials and traditional joinery techniques.
www.harveyjones.com

Page 120 top row, centre row left and centre, bottom row centre and right; page 202 bottom left: **Sycamore Lighting** are a leading trade supplier of kitchen, bathroom, bedroom and specification lighting. Their extensive portfolio includes plinth lights, cabinet lights, illuminated shelves, illuminated mirrors and energy saving lighting.
Tel: +44 (0) 1132 866686;
www.sycamorelightingltd.co.uk

Page 120 middle row far right, bottom row left; page 168 bottom row left and second left: **THG Stainless Steel systems** offers loose lay floor clip tiles in 10 standard designs, complimentary wall tiles and special fabrication of splash-backs. Bespoke pattern designs are also available. They also offer Solid & Engineered Wood flooring, Rubber, Luxury Vinyl planks & tiles and Porcelain Clip floor & wall tiles.
Tel: +44 (0) 2076 028057;
www.thginternational.co.uk

Page 168 bottom row far right; page 169 third row centre, bottom row nos 1 2 & 4 from left; page 176 bottom row nos 2 3 & 4 from left: **Byrock** is an influential supplier of New Generation Materials. Their collections are of the highest quality; innovative products sourced world wide.
Tel: +44 (0) 2074 488880;
www.byrock.co.uk

Page 169 top row left and third from left, third row far right; page 176 middle row far left: **Ted Todd and Sons** are an FSC certified timber flooring company based in the UK whose success is built on unique flooring designs, sustainably sourced with high performance levels for classic and contemporary interiors.
Tel: +44 (0) 1925 283011;
www.tedtodd.co.uk

Page 169 top row far right, second row second from right: **Tabu** parquets combine the traditional characteristics of a parquet with the advantages of multi-laminar wood: a better performance, greater density and resistance, very short installation times and easy maintenance.
www.tabu.it

Page 151 far right; page 168 third row far left and second left; page 179 top; page 192 top right: **Stone Age** is a specialist supplier of natural stone, catering for all aspects of kitchens including floors, worktops, splash backs and basins.
Tel: +44 (0) 2073 849040;
www.stone-age.co.uk

Page 176 top row, second row second and fourth from left, bottom row far left: Art Diffusion Panels by **Interlam** are high end decorative HDF panels, curved or sculpted into dramatic organic forms with CNC routers. The range of uses for this product is enormous – decorating the walls of a lobby with art, converted to furniture or simply covering a floor to ceiling wall to enhance its aesthetic appeal.
www.naa.ie

Page 176 middle row second from the right: **Elitis** produces a collection of ultra glossy washable, varnished, impact resistant, sculptural wall vinyl designs for private customers and the contract market. www.elitis.fr

Page 192 bottom right; page 203 top left, bottom row right and left: **Simply Italian UK Ltd** are suppliers of contemporary Italian interiors to the contract industry including architects, specifiers and developers. They specialise in storage solutions, contract seating and finest marble, offering design, supply and installation services.
Tel: +44 (0) 2070 958485;
www.simply-italian.co.uk

Editorial Director Jane O'Shea
Designer Stafford Cliff
Photographer Christian Sarramon
Design Assistant Katherine Case
Editor Simon Davis
Production Vincent Smith,
Marina Asenjo

This paperback edition first published in 2010 by
Quadrille Publishing Limited
Alhambra House
27–31 Charing Cross Road
London WC2H 0LS
www.quadrille.co.uk

Design and layout © 2009
Quadrille Publishing Limited
Photography © 2009 Christian Sarramon
Text © 2009 Stafford Cliff

Cataloguing in Publication Data: a catalogue record for this book is available from the British Library.

ISBN: 978 184400 834 6

Printed in China